GREAT WHITE SHARKS

by Josh Gregory

Children's Press®

An Imprint of Scholastic Inc.
New York Toronto London Auckland Sydney
Mexico City New Delhi Hong Kong
Danbury, Connecticut

Content Consultant
Dr. Stephen S. Ditchkoff
Professor of Wildlife Sciences
Auburn University
Auburn, Alabama

Photographs © 2014: age fotostock/Tom Campbell: 39; Alamy Images: 24 (Dan Callister), 7 (Photoshot Holdings Ltd.), 32 (Reinhard Dirscherl); AP Images/Monterey County Herald, Vern Fisher: 28; Bob Italiano: 44 foreground, 45 foreground; Getty Images: cover, 12 (David Yarrow Photography), 5 top, 16 (Stephen Frink), 27 (Visuals Unlimited, Inc./David Fleetham); Media Bakery: 4, 5 background, 15, 23; Science Source: 31 (Christian Darkin), 5 bottom, 36, 40 (Jeff Rotman); Shutterstock, Inc.: 2, 3, 44 background, 45 background (aqua4), 11 (Jim Agronick); Superstock, Inc.: 35 (age fotostock), 19 (imagebroker.net), 1, 8, 46 (Minden Pictures), 20 (NaturePL).

Library of Congress Cataloging-in-Publication Data
Gregory, Josh.
Great white sharks / by Josh Gregory.
pages cm.–(Nature's children)
Includes bibliographical references and index.
ISBN 978-0-531-23359-7 (lib. bdg.) – ISBN 978-0-531-25157-7 (pbk.)
1. White shark–Juvenile literature. I. Title.
QL638.95.L3G765 2013
597.3'3–dc23 2013000104

Printed in China 62

2 3 4 5 6 7 8 9 10 R 23 22 21 20 19 18 17 16 15 14

FACT FILE

Great White Sharks

Class	Chondrichthyes
Order	Lamniformes
Family	*Lamnidae*
Genus	*Carcharodon*
Species	*Carcharodon carcharias*
World distribution	Found in all nonpolar oceans
Habitats	Temperate, tropical, and subtropical ocean waters, especially near coastlines
Distinctive physical characteristics	Smooth skin; camouflage coloring with gray on top, white on belly; powerful jaws with sharp teeth; strong tail; skeleton made of cartilage
Habits	Swims constantly, usually staying near the coast; territorial, especially of hunting areas; female carries fertilized eggs until they are hatched, giving birth to live young
Diet	Primarily eats seals and sea lions; also known to eat other sea animals, including fish and squid; sometimes scavenges meat from whale carcasses

Contents

CHAPTER 1

Underwater Warriors

A group of huge, heavy elephant seals swims through the warm waters off the coast of Southern California. Rays of sunlight shine down from above. Below the seals lie the murky depths of the Pacific Ocean. Little do the seals know that a threatening **predator** swims beneath them, preparing to strike.

Along the rear of the group, a male seal keeps watch for enemies. Even with his senses on alert, the seal is taken by surprise as a massive set of jaws emerges from the darkness below. The jaws snap shut around his belly. The great white shark has made another successful kill! As razor-sharp teeth tear into the unlucky seal, the rest of the group swims off into the distance. The shark is left to settle in for a tasty meal.

Great white sharks often burst up from below to attack seals and other animals swimming near the surface of the ocean.

Sizable Sharks

The great white shark's reputation as a ferocious hunter is well earned. This powerful predator lies at the top of the ocean food chain. This means that it is free to roam the world's waters in search of prey. It doesn't have to worry that another animal might attack it.

One factor that makes the great white shark so dangerous is its incredible size. It is not the largest shark in the world, but it is the largest shark that regularly eats meat. An average great white shark is between 16 and 20 feet (4.9 and 6.1 meters) long. It weighs between 4,000 and 7,000 pounds (1,814 and 3,175 kilograms). One of the largest ever recorded was around 21 feet (6.4 m) long. The huge animal weighed 7,300 pounds (3,311 kg). That is heavier than the combined weight of two cars.

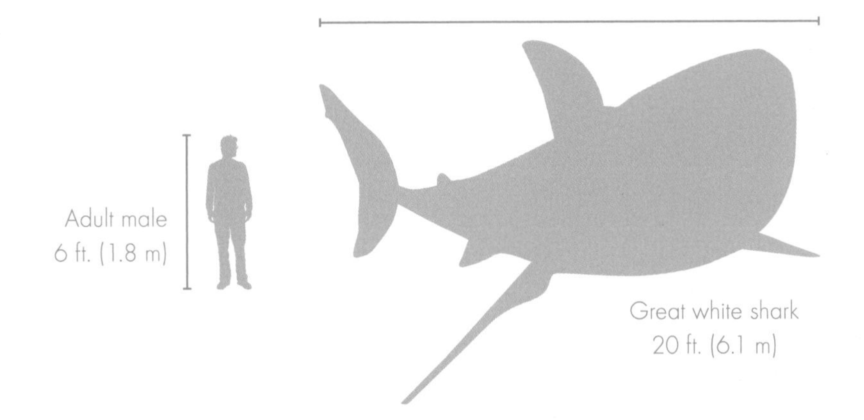

Most of a great white shark's weight comes from its powerful muscles.

Kings of the Ocean

Great white sharks are found throughout most of the world's oceans, living everywhere except the coldest areas. They especially favor **temperate** waters. Great whites hunt for prey from the surface down to depths of 4,400 feet (1,341 m). These sharks are most often found near coastlines. They are especially common in the waters of the Pacific Ocean near California and Mexico and in the Indian Ocean near South Africa and Australia.

Great white sharks are an extremely important part of the ocean **ecosystem**. As top predators, they keep the populations of other **marine** animals in check. Though the sharks are found almost everywhere, there are less than 3,500 of them in the world. This means they are very spread out. Only a small number of great whites might be found in any one area.

After a filling meal, a great white shark can go days or even weeks before eating again.

CHAPTER 2

Hunting in the Depths

As some of the most dangerous hunters in the ocean, great white sharks eat a wide variety of prey. The main staples of an adult great white's diet are seals and sea lions. These large marine mammals have thick layers of fat called **blubber** beneath their skin. Blubber gives sharks a huge boost of nutrients. This provides them the energy they need to stay on the move. When they can't find seals or sea lions, the sharks are more than happy to eat other animals. Fish, turtles, otters, and small whales are just a few examples. Sometimes they even eat other sharks, including smaller great whites.

A shark's diet depends on its size. Younger sharks are not large enough to take on seals or sea lions. Instead they stick to smaller prey such as fish and rays. Larger great white sharks are known to eat **carrion**. Dead whales provide an easy source of nutritious blubber.

Seals have been known to fight back during a great white shark attack, sometimes leaving scars on its attacker.

Sneak Attack

The great white shark is known for its coloring. The shark's upper body is light gray, and its underside is creamy white. It is this white coloring that earned the species its name. This distinctive appearance is about more than just looks, though. It provides **camouflage** to help the shark sneak up on unsuspecting prey. A shark's gray upper body blends in with the dark color of the ocean below. Its white belly matches the bright light that shines down from above the surface. As a result, it's hard for potential prey to see the shark from above or below.

A great white shark takes advantage of this by relying on surprise attacks when it hunts. When it spots a target, the shark opens its jaws wide and makes a sudden lunge from below. The shark chomps down as the prey enters its mouth. If the shark misses on the first attack, the prey might get away. If the shark succeeds, the prey quickly bleeds to death.

Great white sharks swim near the ocean surface as they search for prey.

Mighty Mouths

A shark's mouth is its most important hunting tool. When preparing to strike, the shark opens its mouth wide. It does this by lowering its bottom jaw and lifting its top jaw at the same time. The upper jaw sticks out from the shark's **snout**, exposing its gums. As the shark wraps its gaping mouth around an unlucky animal, it raises the lower jaw first to trap the prey. Then it brings its upper jaw down to take a bite.

The shark's deadly teeth also play an important role in killing prey. The teeth on the bottom jaw are narrow and pointy to grasp captured prey. The teeth on the top jaw are wider to cut away chunks of meat to swallow. All of a great white shark's teeth are **serrated**, making them even more deadly. As the shark ages, it routinely loses its teeth. New ones grow in to replace them.

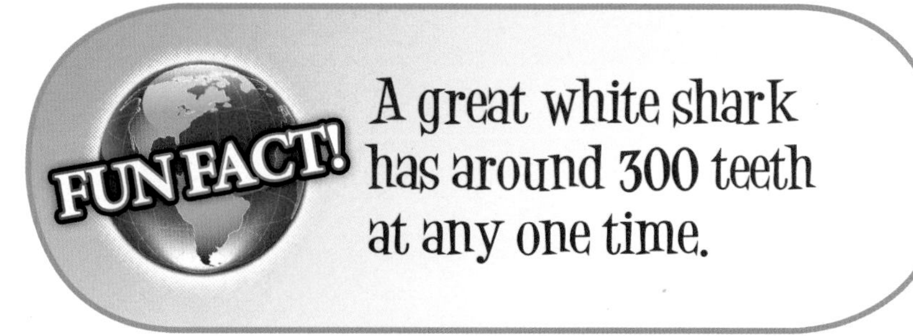

Great white sharks can move both their upper and lower jaws. Many other animals, including humans, move only their lower jaw.

Shaped for Success

The vast majority of fish species have bony skeletons. Sharks are different. A shark's skeleton is all **cartilage**, except for its jaw. This type of skeleton is called cartilaginous. Cartilage weighs less than regular bones. It is also more flexible. This helps sharks to maneuver quickly and easily through the water.

Great white sharks have very powerful muscles, especially in their jaws and tails. The jaw muscles give the sharks their powerful bite. Their tail muscles help them speed through the ocean. The muscles that a shark uses to swim sometimes connect directly to the inside of its skin. This allows the shark to use less energy when swimming.

A great white shark's skin acts as a sort of outer skeleton. Like other cartilaginous fish, a shark has smooth rather than scaly skin. This helps the shark glide through the water with little resistance to slow it down.

A great white shark's tough skin is often covered in bite marks and other scars.

A Hunter's Senses

Great white sharks locate prey using sharp senses. Their most powerful sense is smell. A shark can detect a drop of blood in 25 gallons (95 liters) of water. Great whites have been known to smell blood from as far as 3 miles (5 kilometers) away.

Another important sense is taste. Taste buds cover the inside of the shark's mouth and throat. The shark uses its taste buds to identify different kinds of food before swallowing. This helps the shark find the most nutritious parts of its prey.

A shark's eye is divided into two sections. One allows the shark to see during the day. The other is used at night and in dark areas of the ocean. This means that the shark has clear vision in almost any light condition.

Even though great white sharks have very small ears, they can hear very well. The tiny holes located behind the shark's eyes can detect underwater sounds from miles away.

Great white sharks hear low-pitched sounds better than they hear high-pitched ones.

Special Senses

Like all fish, great white sharks have a lateral line. The lateral line runs along the shark's back from its head to its tail. It contains many powerful sensory cells, which make the shark very sensitive to vibrations in the water. When another animal swims nearby, the shark can tell how far away it is and in which direction it is moving. The shark can even notice these things from up to 820 feet (250 m) away.

Sharks also have a special sense that humans and most other animals lack. Special cells in a shark's snout can detect electrical fields in the water. These cells are called ampullae of Lorenzini. Because all living things produce small amounts of electricity, this sense helps sharks locate prey. It also helps them navigate through the ocean by enabling them to detect the earth's magnetic fields.

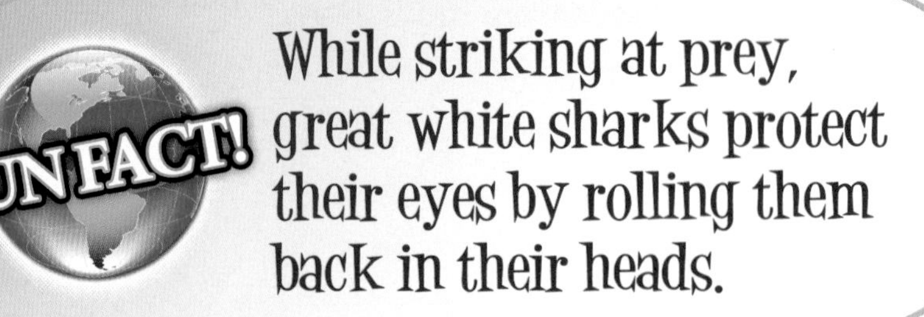

Ampullae of Lorenzini can help sharks find prey that is buried under sand or otherwise out of sight.

Always on the Move

Thanks to their strong, **streamlined** bodies, great white sharks are excellent swimmers. They can reach speeds of up to 35 miles (56 km) per hour. They can even launch themselves completely out of the water when snatching prey. A shark's tail propels it forward. A series of fins allows the shark to make quick turns.

Sharks never stop moving. Like all fish, sharks breathe using **gills**. As the shark swims, water moves through its mouth. The gills filter out from the water the oxygen that the shark needs to live. If the shark is forced to stop moving, water stops flowing through its gills. Then the shark would eventually die.

Scientists aren't sure if great white sharks ever get a chance to rest. Some scientists believe that the sharks can enter a kind of sleep when they need to, while continuing to swim.

Great white sharks can launch their bodies completely out of the water. This is called breaching.

CHAPTER 3

Shark Life

Because sharks live in the ocean and move around a lot, scientists have a hard time studying how these amazing predators live. As a result, not much is known about the sharks' social interactions. They are mostly solitary animals, though they occasionally travel in pairs. Great white sharks can be territorial, especially in hunting areas.

One of the few times great white sharks approach each other is when it comes time to mate. Few people have seen great white sharks mate in the wild. Scientists are unsure of the sharks' courtship process. However, experts believe that males often bite females to hold them in place during mating. Scars commonly found on the bodies of females support this idea. Most fish lay eggs after mating. But female great white sharks carry the fertilized eggs inside their bodies until it is time for the babies to be born.

Though most great white sharks prefer to live alone, pairs have sometimes been known to travel together for long periods of time.

Predatory Pups

Around 12 months after mating, the mother shark heads toward warm waters to give birth. The eggs hatch inside the mother's body. Then the baby sharks make their way out into the ocean. A great white shark **litter** usually consists of between 2 and 10 pups. The average newborn pup is around 3.3 feet (1 m) long. Pups are born fully formed and ready to hunt. They sometimes even eat each other before leaving their mother's body. Once born, the pups swim away immediately. The mother does not provide care or protection for her young, but special **hormones** do keep her from eating the pups.

As pups, great white sharks are vulnerable to attacks from larger fish, including adult great white sharks. Such attacks become less of a risk as the young sharks grow. Once male great white sharks are around 10 years old, they can begin producing young of their own. Females are usually not ready to mate until they are slightly older.

This young great white shark, temporarily held at an aquarium in California, was fed chunks of salmon and other fish during its stay.

CHAPTER 4

Past and Present Predators

Sharks have been swimming Earth's oceans for a very long time. Fossils show that their earliest ancestors lived more than 450 million years ago. That makes them even older than dinosaurs! One early shark species was *Cladoselache*. This ancient fish lived around 370 million years ago. It swam through waters covering the area that is now the states of Tennessee, Ohio, and Kentucky. Scientists believe that it captured prey by simply swimming very fast and swallowing slower fish whole.

Sharks similar to the ones living today first appeared around 100 million years ago. This is around the time dinosaurs roamed the land. The megalodon first appeared around 65 million to 60 million years ago, as the dinosaurs died out. This great white shark ancestor is one of the largest shark species that ever lived. It grew to lengths of 45 feet (13.7 m) and ate large whales.

Because shark skeletons are mostly cartilage, they don't fossilize as well as bony animals.

So Many Sharks

Ancient species such as the megalodon are now **extinct**. However, there are more than 400 shark species living today. The largest living shark species, and the largest of all living fish species, is the whale shark. This massive shark averages around 39 feet (12 m) in length. It weighs around 15 tons (14 metric tons). Despite its incredible size, it eats only small creatures such as fish and **plankton**. Instead of hunting, it lives by filter feeding. This means that it swims with its mouth open, allowing water and anything floating in it to stream inside. The water pours out through the shark's gills, leaving plankton and fish behind.

The smallest shark species is the dwarf lantern shark. This tiny shark averages just 8 inches (20 centimeters) long. It is found swimming in the depths of the Caribbean Sea. Like many deep-sea creatures, it is capable of making its body light up.

Whale sharks are most often found in warm tropical ocean waters.

Close Cousins

Two fish that are closely related to sharks are skates and rays. Skates and rays are very similar to each other, and it can be difficult to tell them apart. Both have wide, flat bodies and long tails. One main difference between them is that rays have longer, thinner tails. The tails often end in stinging spines that the rays use to defend themselves. Skates have shorter, thicker tails and cannot sting. Rays also tend to be larger than skates. The largest ray species, the manta ray, can be up to 30 feet (9.1 m) wide! But the largest skate, the common skate, grows to be just 8.2 feet (2.5 m) wide on average.

Rays can be very dangerous to humans. They can whip their tails around with tremendous speed, jabbing unsuspecting swimmers with the spine at the end. This can cause large wounds. **Venom** on the spines often causes infection. Some rays can also defend themselves by releasing an electrical charge into the water.

Manta rays sometimes leap out of the water, possibly to remove parasites, attract a mate, or just to play.

CHAPTER 5

Sharing the Seas with Sharks

Great white sharks have been saddled with a fearsome reputation over the years. Movies such as *Jaws* portray them as ruthless killing machines on the hunt for a meal of humans. This unfair view of great white sharks can be traced back to 1916. That year, great white sharks attacked five people over the course of several days along the coast of New Jersey. Though these attacks were likely the work of a single shark showing strange behavior, word soon spread that great white sharks were a major danger to humans.

While sharks do sometimes attack people and can cause serious injuries, they are not a very big threat overall. There are usually around 30 to 50 great white shark attacks each year. Only around one per year actually results in death. The truth is that great white sharks are not interested in eating people. They would much rather go hunting for tasty, blubbery seals and sea lions.

Though great white sharks may not go out of their way to hunt humans, it's a good idea for divers to play it safe when swimming with sharks.

A Deadly Disappearance

Believe it or not, humans are a much bigger danger to great white sharks than the sharks are to them. Millions of sharks are killed every year in commercial fishing operations. Their meat is especially prized in Japan. There, a shark's fin is an ingredient in a popular soup. Some fishers are known to cut the fins off captured sharks and then dump the rest of the body back in the water. This process is known as finning, and it leaves the sharks unable to swim. They either sink and drown, or their bodies are washed ashore by waves.

Sharks must also contend with damage to their ocean **habitat**. Humans often dump waste in and near the ocean. This can be poisonous to ocean life, including the animals that sharks rely on for food. As these animals slowly disappear, there is less for sharks to eat.

Sometimes great white sharks are accidentally killed when they become trapped in fishing nets.

Saving the Sharks

Because of overfishing and other human activities, the worldwide great white shark population is shrinking. However, some **conservationists** and governments are working to keep these amazing hunters from disappearing. In some parts of the world, including Australia and South Africa, great white sharks are protected by law. In 2012, the U.S. government began investigating whether the sharks should be protected as an **endangered** species. Conservationists are also working to make finning illegal in the United States.

To keep sharks safe, people need to understand the important role these fish play in maintaining the ocean ecosystem. People should also understand that sharks mean them no harm. As this information spreads, more people will join in the struggle to save the sharks. With a little help, these ferocious fish will prowl the world's oceans for many years to come.

A photographer attempts to photograph the inside of a great white's mouth as an expert tickles the shark, encouraging it to open its jaws.

Words to Know

ancestors (AN-ses-turz) — ancient animal species that are related to modern species

blubber (BLUHB-ur) — the layer of fat under the skin of a whale, seal, or other large marine mammal

camouflage (KAM-uh-flahzh) — coloring or body shape that allows an animal to blend in with its surroundings

carrion (KAR-ee-uhn) — dead and putrefying flesh

cartilage (KAR-tuh-lij) — a strong elastic tissue

conservationists (kon-sur-VAY-shun-ists) — people who work to protect an environment and the living things in it

courtship (KORT-ship) — the process in which an animal expresses its interest in mating

ecosystem (EE-koh-sis-tuhm) — all the living things in a place and their relation to the environment

endangered (en-DAYN-jurd) — at risk of becoming extinct, usually because of human activity

extinct (ik-STINGKT) — no longer found alive

fertilized (FUR-tuh-lizd) — joined with sperm cells from a male

fossils (FAH-suhlz) — a bone, shell, or other trace of an animal or plant from millions of years ago, preserved as rock

gills (GILZ) — organs near a fish's mouth through which it breathes by extracting oxygen from water

habitat (HAB-uh-tat) — the place where an animal or a plant is usually found

hormones (HOR-mohnz) — chemical substances made by the body that affect growth, development, and behavior

lateral line (LAH-tuh-rul LINE) — a sense organ found on the side of the body that sharks use to detect vibrations and changes in water pressure

litter (LIT-ur) — a group of baby animals that are born at the same time to the same mother

marine (muh-REEN) — of or having to do with the ocean

plankton (PLANGK-tun) — tiny animals and plants that drift or float in oceans and lakes

predator (PRED-uh-tur) — an animal that lives by hunting other animals for food

prey (PRAY) — an animal that's hunted by another animal for food

sensory (SENS-or-ee) — of or having to do with the powers a living being uses to learn about its surroundings

serrated (SER-ay-tid) — having a jagged edge like that of a saw

snout (SNOUT) — the long front part of an animal's head, including the nose, mouth, and jaws

solitary (SAH-li-ter-ee) — not requiring or without the companionship of others

streamlined (STREEM-lined) — shaped to minimize resistance to water

temperate (TEM-pur-it) — having a climate where the temperature is rarely very high or very low

territorial (terr-uh-TOR-ee-uhl) — defensive of a certain area

venom (VEN-uhm) — poison produced by some animals

Habitat Map

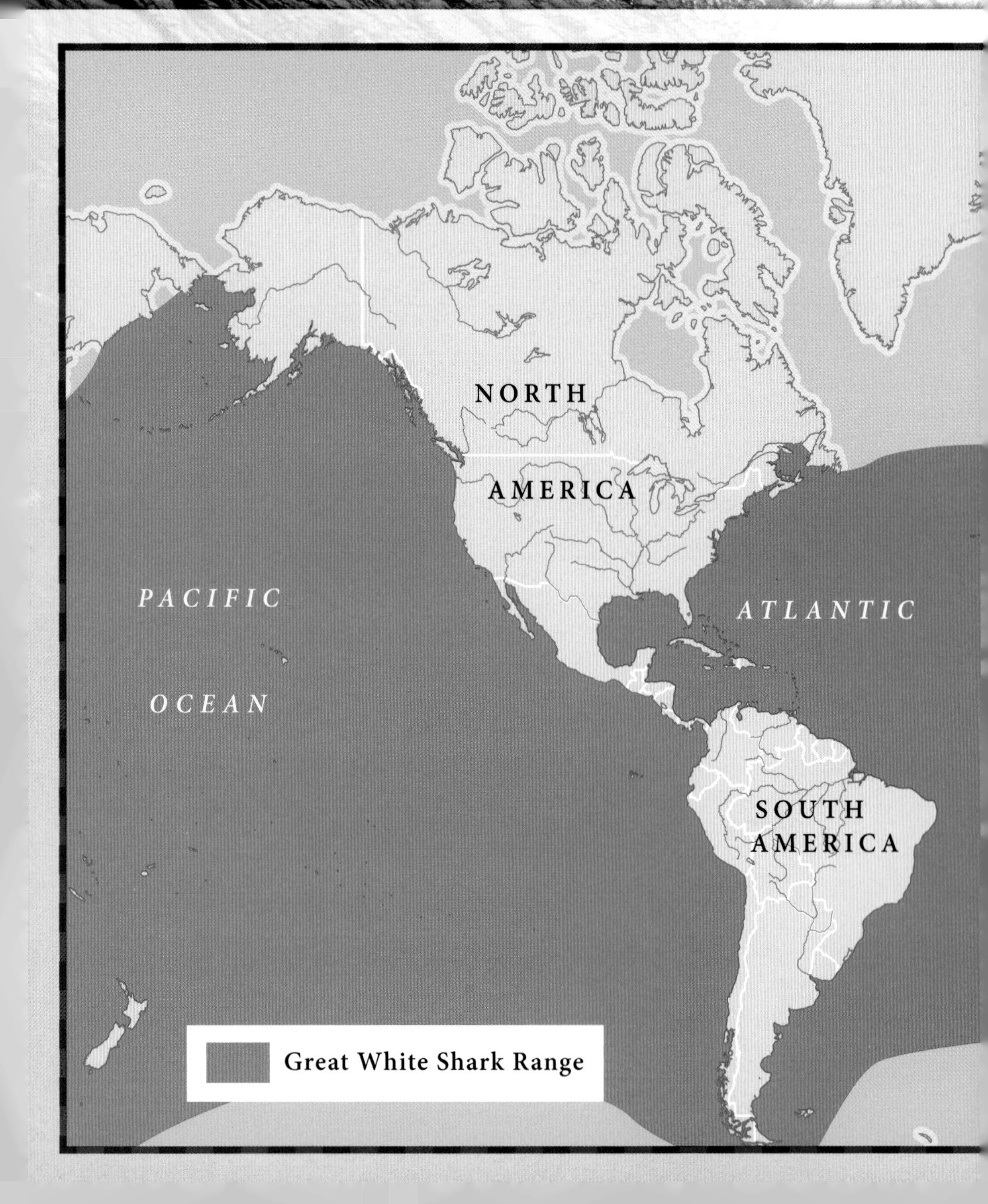
NORTH
AMERICA
PACIFIC
OCEAN
ATLANTIC
SOUTH
AMERICA
Great White Shark Range

ARCTIC OCEAN
EUROPE
ASIA
AFRICA
PACIFIC OCEAN
INDIAN OCEAN
OCEAN
AUSTRALIA

Find Out More

Books

Doubilet, David, and Jennifer Hayes. *Face to Face with Sharks*. Washington, DC: National Geographic, 2009.

Musgrave, Ruth. *National Geographic Kids Everything Sharks*. Washington, DC: National Geographic, 2011.

Owings, Lisa. *The Great White Shark*. Minneapolis: Bellwether Media, 2012.

Reynolds, Hunter. *Hunting with Great White Sharks*. New York: Gareth Stevens, 2013.

Visit this Scholastic Web site for more information on great white sharks:
www.factsfornow.scholastic.com
Enter the keywords **Great White Sharks**

Index

Page numbers in *italics* indicate a photograph or map.

(Index continued)

About the Author

Josh Gregory writes and edits books for kids. He lives in Chicago, Illinois.